This book belongs to:

tiger tales

5 River Road, Suite 128, Wilton, CT 06897

Published in the United States 2021

Text by Lauren Crisp

Photographic images courtesy of www.shutterstock.com

ISBN-13: 978-1-6643-4007-7

ISBN-10: 1-6643-4007-6

Printed in China

LTK/1800/0937/0920

www.tigertalesbooks.com

Learn to Write

Contents

Introduction for parents and guardians

Learn to Write is a workbook designed to build your child's confidence and ability in writing skills from a young age, ensuring a solid foundation for their future reading, writing, and comprehension skills. Learning by doing is the key to developing the hand muscles and fine motor skills needed for writing.

This workbook focuses on the formation of lowercase letters, for a few reasons:

- They are easier for little hands to print.

- They are used more frequently in writing.

- Learning both lowercase and capital letters at the same time can be overwhelming.

Capital letters and numbers are introduced in brief toward the end of the workbook.

The workbook is organized alphabetically, but there is no set order that needs to be followed. You can even choose to have your child learn to write by focusing on letter families—letters that are formed by using similar patterns and strokes. Please see page 6 for more about this approach.

Have fun! Talk with your child about each activity; encourage him or her; and ask questions. Allow breaks when necessary. And don't forget to present your child with the certificate of achievement when the workbook is complete!

Letter families

Your child can learn to write by becoming familiar with the four letter families: curly letters, anchor letters, elevator letters, and zigzag letters.

The letters in each family are formed using similar patterns and strokes. Once your child is comfortable forming one letter, writing the others in that family follows quite easily.

The letters in each family are listed below, starting with the simplest letter and building up to the most complex. If you choose this approach, look for the corresponding symbols and colors on the borders of pages 14 through 65.

 ## Curly letters
(c, a, d, g, q, o, e, s, f)

These letters, best represented by the letter "c," are simple to form. They all begin in the same way, curling around counterclockwise from the top. Sometimes a curly letter has a straight line, too.

 ## Anchor letters
(l, i, t, u, j)

Just like an anchor, these letters start from the top and fall to the bottom. The family is best represented by the letter "l." The more complex anchor letters involve extra strokes.

 ## Elevator letters
(r, n, m, h, b, p)

Best represented by the letter "r," this family is slightly more complicated to form. Just like an elevator, the pencil traces down, before moving back up over the same line and then off in another direction.

 ## Zigzag letters
(z, v, w, x, y, k)

This family is all about straight and diagonal lines, starting with the easiest zigzag, "z," and ending with letters that require some extra strokes. Remember to keep the pencil lines straight!

Learning the basics

HOW TO HOLD A PENCIL

Show your child how to hold a pencil correctly:

- Hold the pencil between the thumb and index finger, with the index finger on top.
- Rest the pencil on the middle finger.
- Rest the side of the hand comfortably on the table.

HOW TO VIEW THE PAGE

Explain to your child that in the English language, we read from left to right, and from the top of the page to the bottom. Be sure the spine of the book is always on the left.

HOW TO USE THE ARROWS, NUMBERS, AND DOTS

This workbook uses a system of dots and numbered arrows to encourage new writers to form each letter correctly.

- Use the black dot on each letter as the starting point for the pencil.

→ Follow the arrows in numerical order.

For letters that require the pencil to leave the page for a second stroke (for example, to cross the letter "t"), this circle indicates the second starting point for the pencil. If a letter does not have this circle, the pencil should not leave the page.

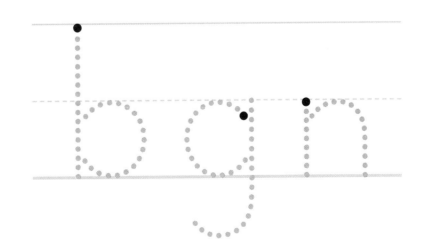

HOW TO USE THE WRITING LINES

On the letter pages, there are three lines to guide writing. The body of the letter should fall within the dotted line and the bottom line.

Drawing curly lines

Trace along these curly lines. Start on the black dot and follow the arrows along the dotted lines.

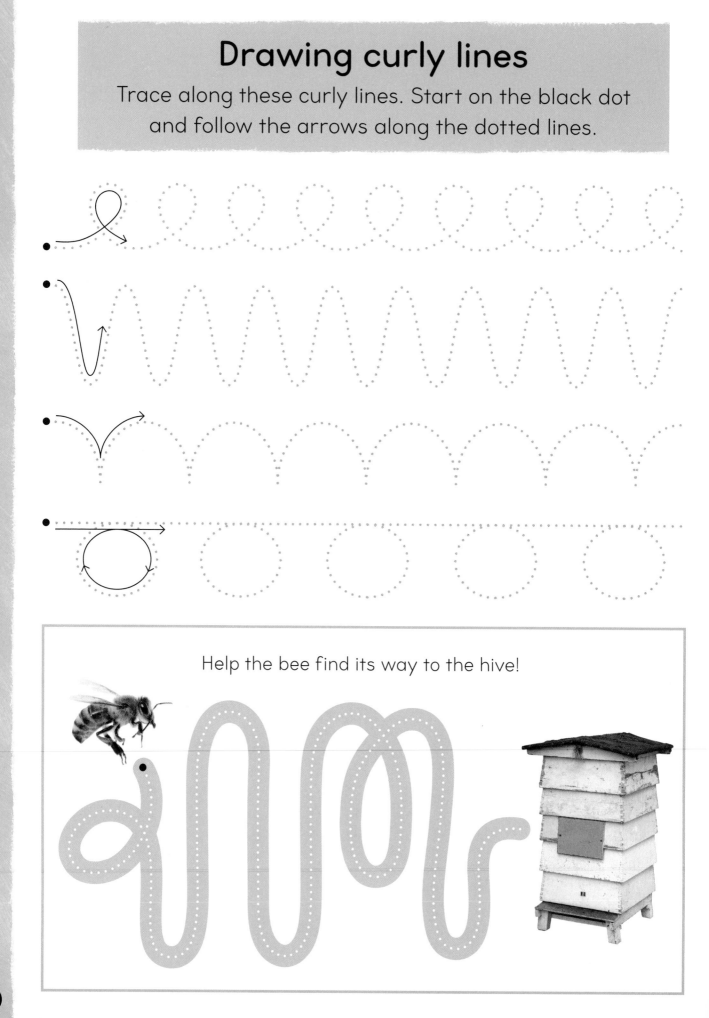

Help the bee find its way to the hive!

Drawing straight lines
Now follow these straight lines.
Keep your pencil nice and steady!

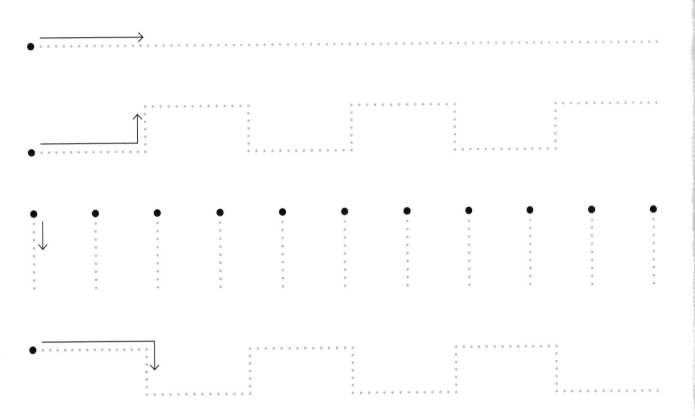

Can you help the kitten find his mommy?

Drawing zigzags

It's zigzag time! Trace up and down diagonally with your pencil.

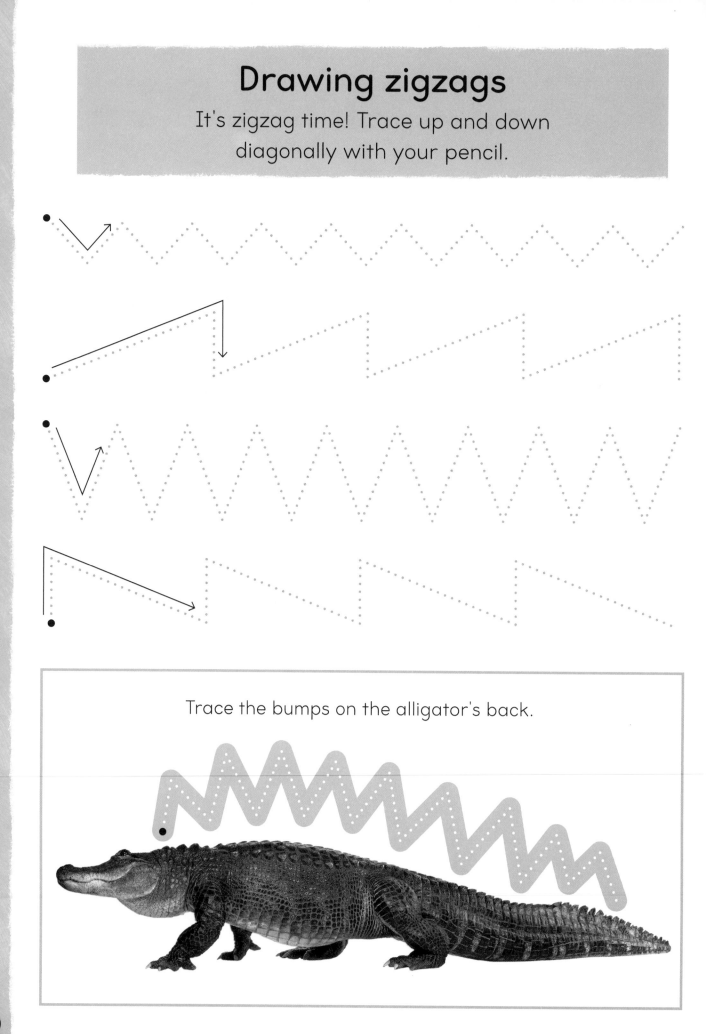

Trace the bumps on the alligator's back.

Can you follow these lines? Some are curly, some are straight, and some are zigzags!

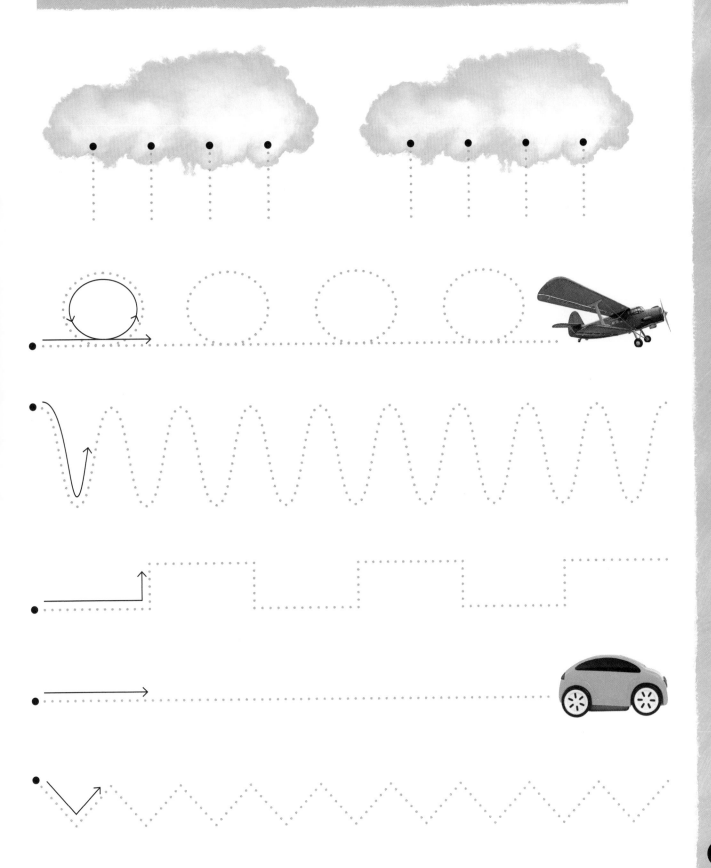

Drawing shapes

Trace these shapes. Once you're finished, color them!

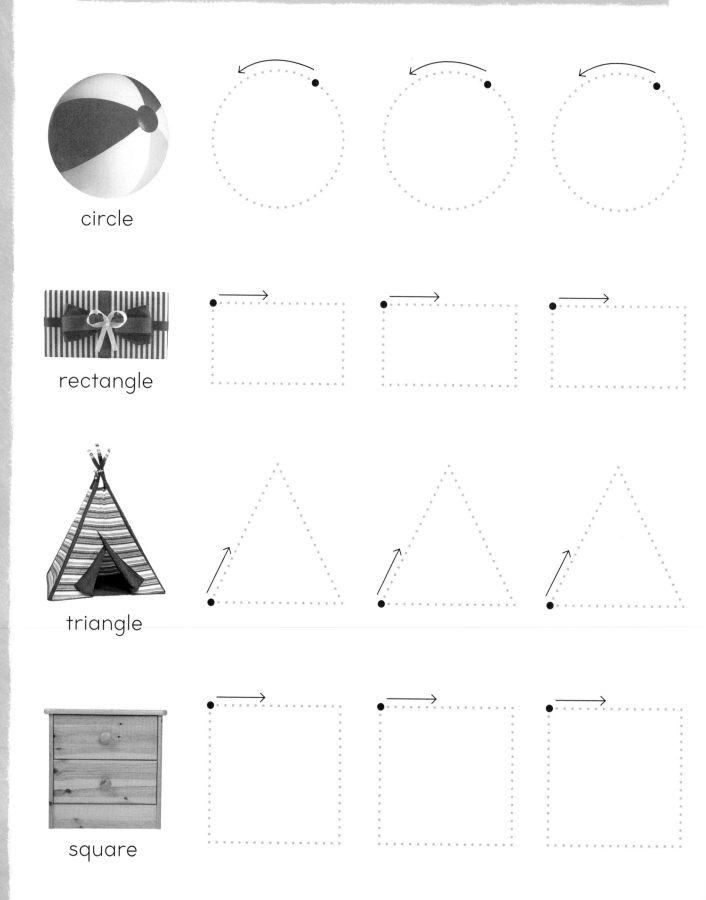

circle

rectangle

triangle

square

Maze fun

Help the puppy find her way through the maze.

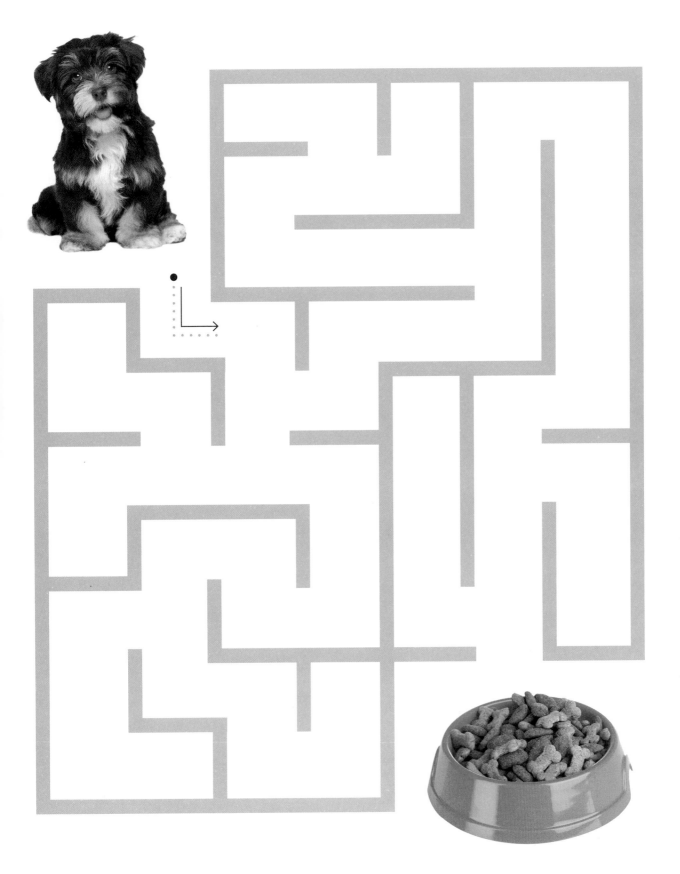

Writing the letter a

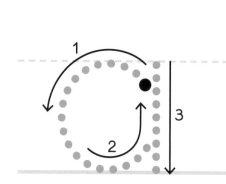

First, trace the letter **a** with your finger. Starting on the black dot, follow the steps below.

1 curl around

2 up to join

3 back down

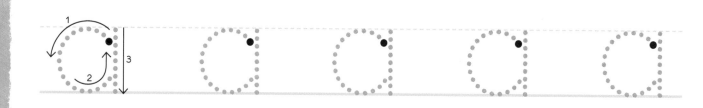

Next, use a pencil to trace the letter **a**.

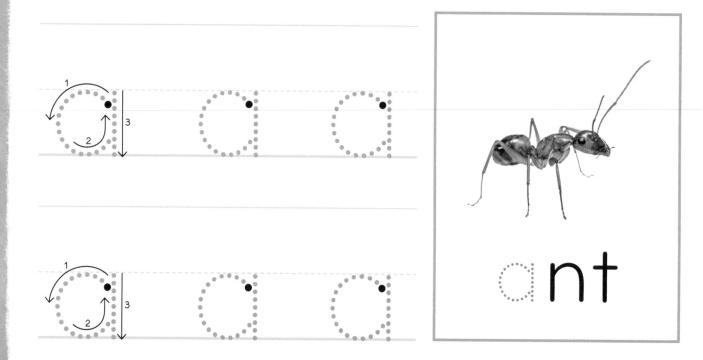

ant

Now, write the letter **a** yourself.

What else begins with **a**?

_pple

alligator   **a**mbulance

Writing the letter **b**

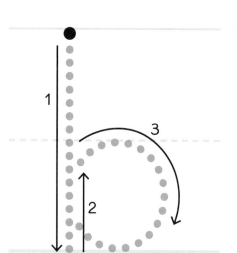

First, trace the letter **b** with your finger. Starting on the black dot, follow the steps below.

1 down

2 back up to the middle

3 around to join

Next, use a pencil to trace the letter **b**.

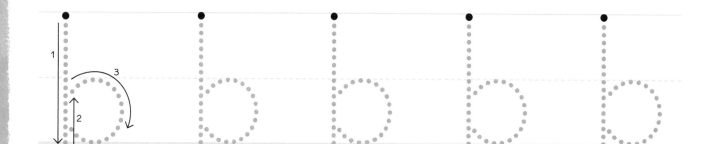

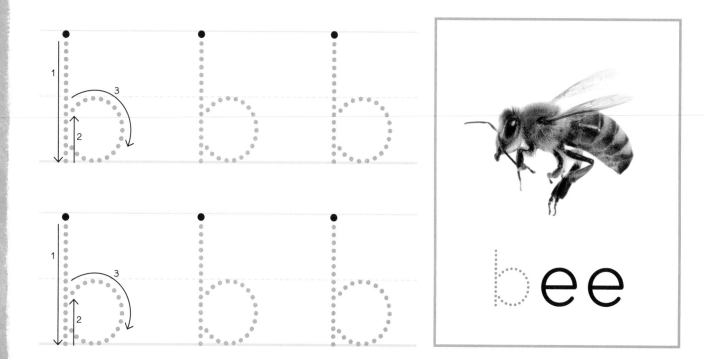

b ee

Now, write the letter **b** yourself.

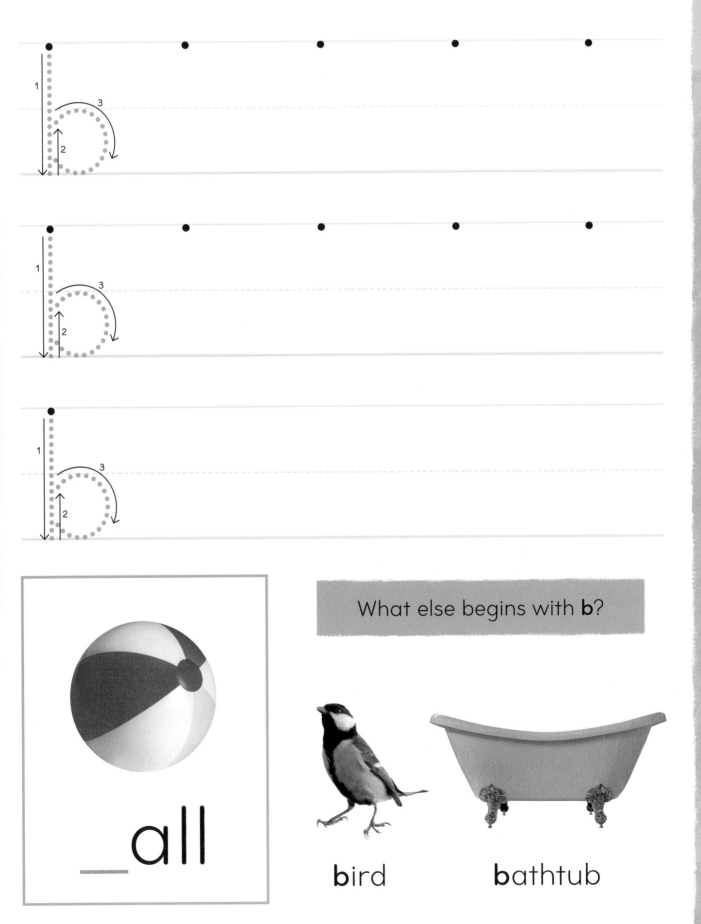

_all

What else begins with **b**?

bird   bathtub

Writing the letter c

First, trace the letter **c** with your finger. Starting on the black dot, follow the steps below.

1 curl around and up

Next, use a pencil to trace the letter **c**.

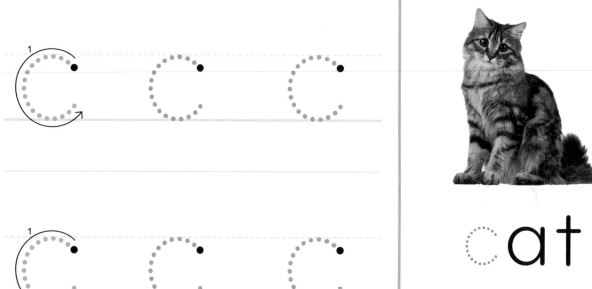

cat

Now, write the letter **c** yourself.

_ar

What else begins with **c**?

carrot   **c**up

Writing the letter **d**

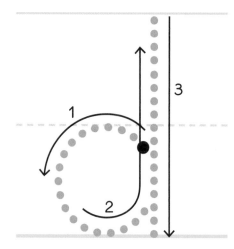

First, trace the letter **d** with your finger. Starting on the black dot, follow the steps below.

1 curl around

2 up to the top

3 back down

Next, use a pencil to trace the letter **d**.

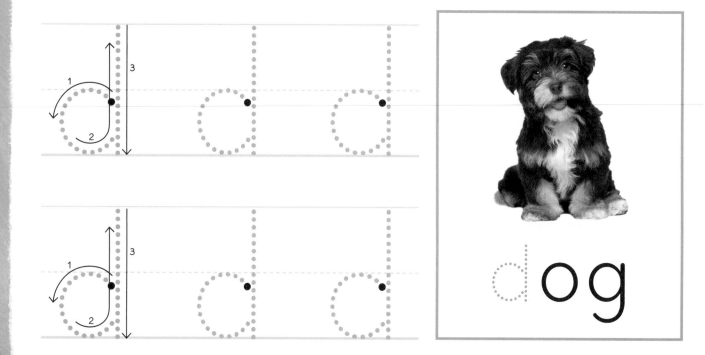

dog

Now, write the letter **d** yourself.

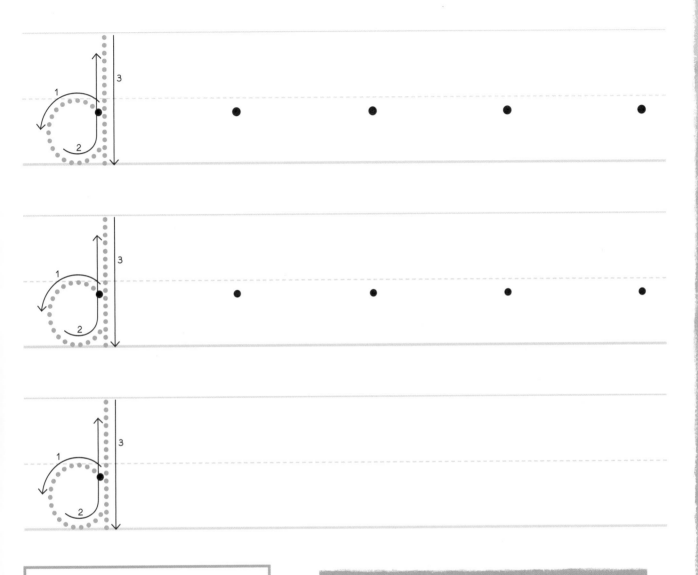

_oll

What else begins with **d**?

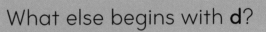

door   **d**rum

Writing the letter e

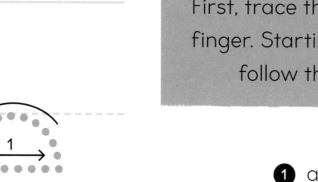

First, trace the letter **e** with your finger. Starting on the black dot, follow the steps below.

1 across

2 curl around and up

Next, use a pencil to trace the letter **e**.

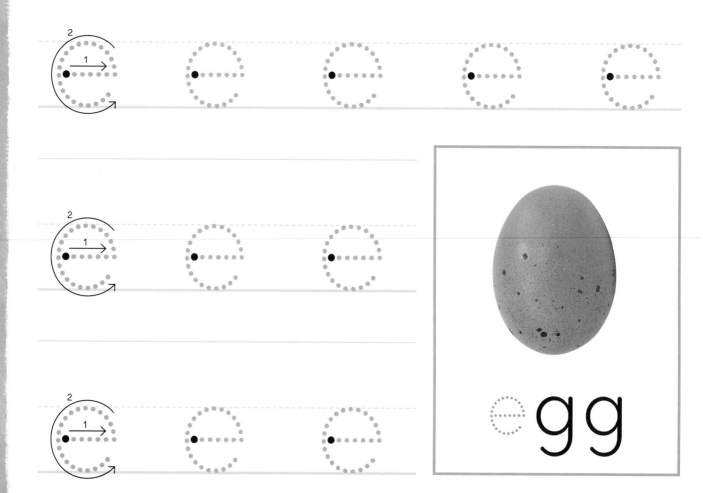

egg

Now, write the letter **e** yourself.

_lephant

What else begins with **e**?

envelope

Writing the letter **f**

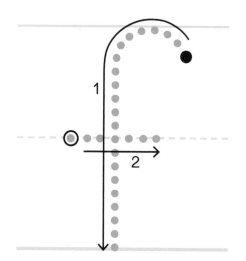

First, trace the letter **f** with your finger. Starting on the black dot, follow the steps below.

1 curl around and down

2 starting a new stroke, follow the arrow across

Next, use a pencil to trace the letter **f**.

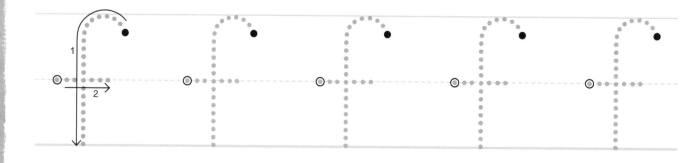

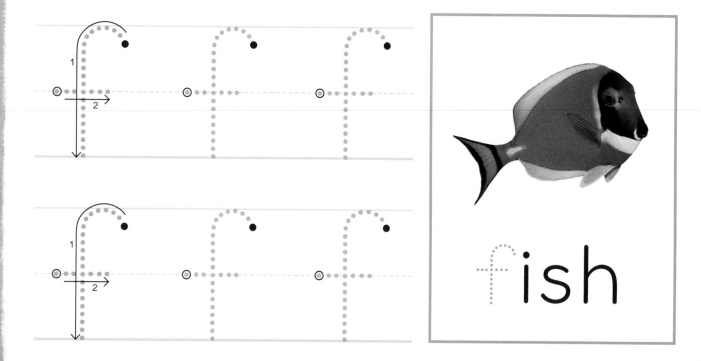

fish

Now, write the letter **f** yourself.

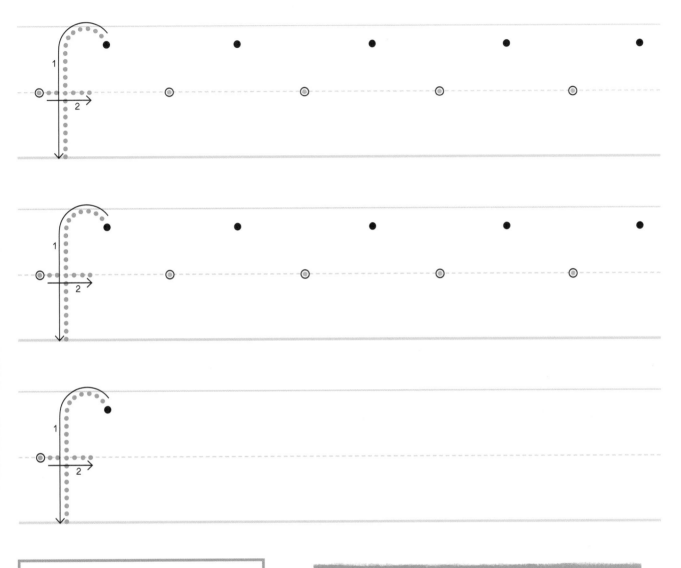

_rog

What else begins with **f**?

flower   fork

Writing the letter g

First, trace the letter **g** with your finger. Starting on the black dot, follow the steps below.

1 curl around

2 up to join

3 back down and around

Next, use a pencil to trace the letter **g**.

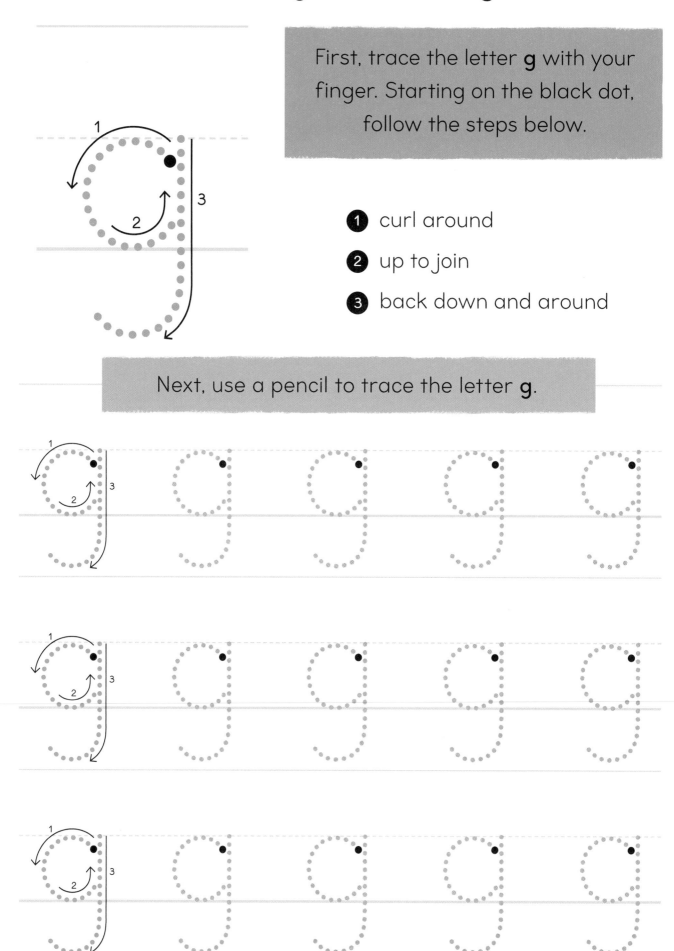

Now, write the letter **g** yourself.

What else begins with **g**?

goat

grass   grapes

Writing the letter **h**

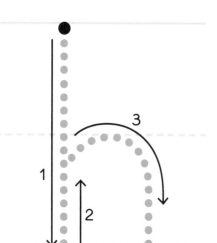

First, trace the letter **h** with your finger. Starting on the black dot, follow the steps below.

1. down
2. back up to the middle
3. around and down

Next, use a pencil to trace the letter **h**.

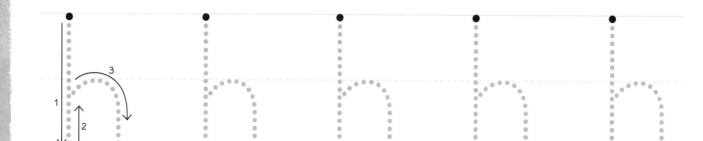

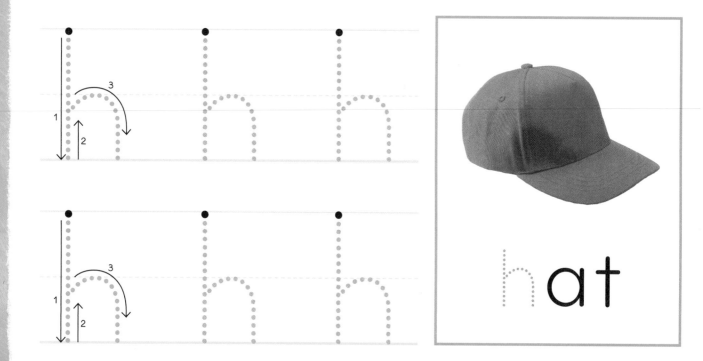

hat

Now, write the letter **h** yourself.

_orse

What else begins with **h**?

hammer   **h**ouse

Writing the letter i

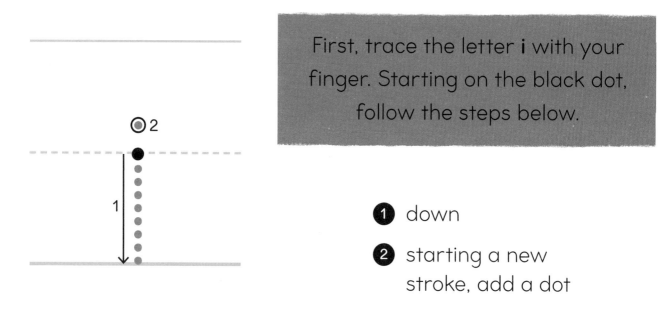

First, trace the letter **i** with your finger. Starting on the black dot, follow the steps below.

1 down

2 starting a new stroke, add a dot

Next, use a pencil to trace the letter **i**.

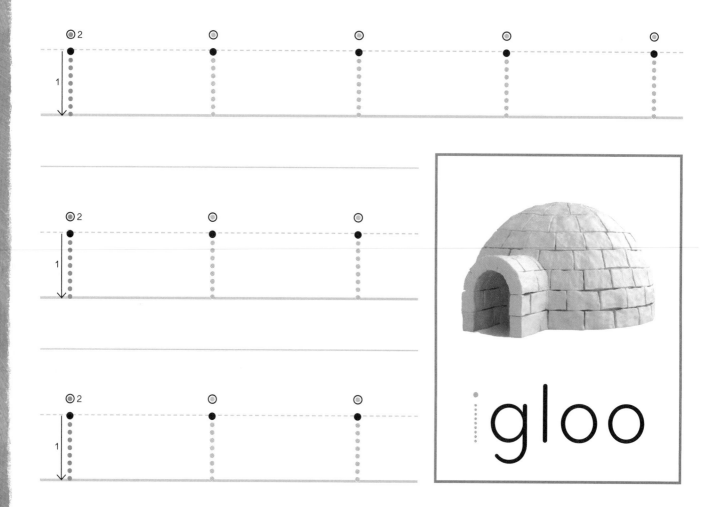

gloo

Now, write the letter **i** yourself.

○ 2
1

○ 2
1

○ 2
1

_nk

What else begins with **i**?

insect

iguana

Writing the letter j

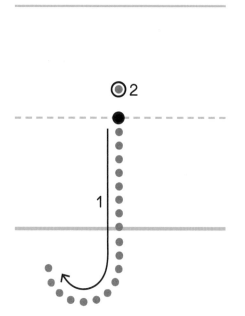

First, trace the letter **j** with your finger. Starting on the black dot, follow the steps below.

1 down and around

2 starting a new stroke, add a dot

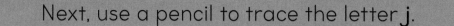

Next, use a pencil to trace the letter **j**.

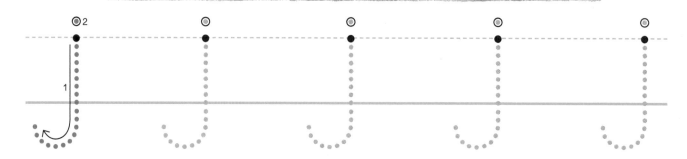

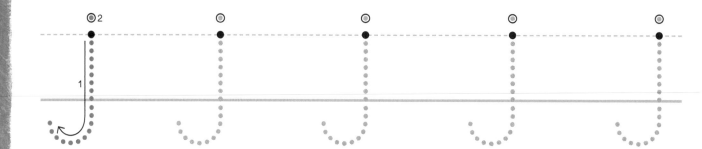

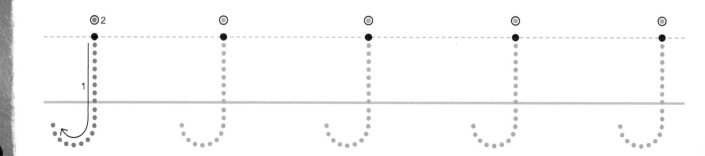

Now, write the letter j yourself.

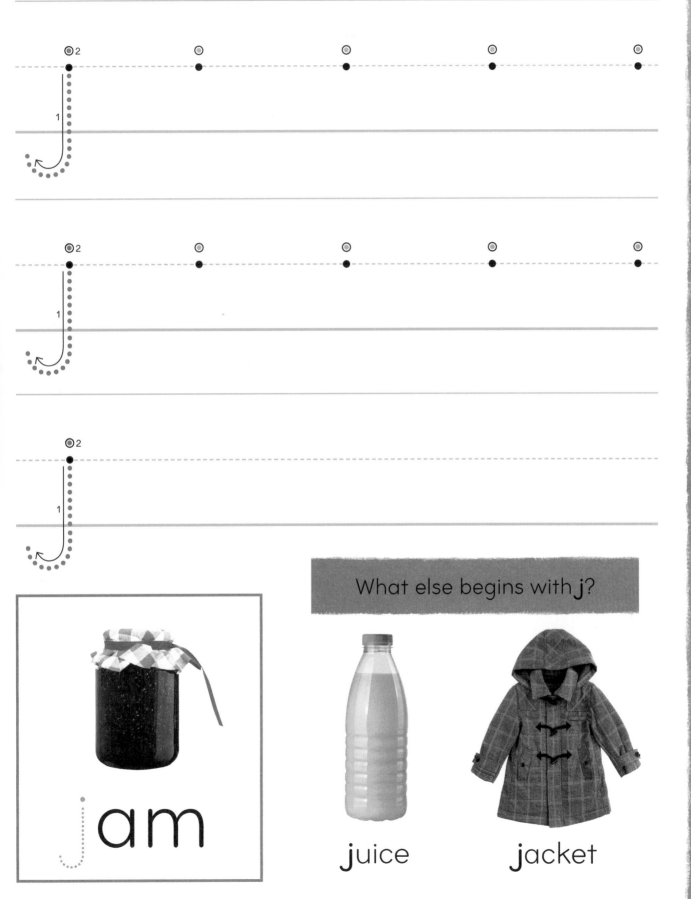

What else begins with j?

jam

juice   jacket

Writing the letter k

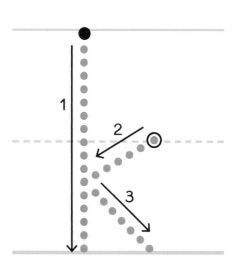

First, trace the letter **k** with your finger. Starting on the black dot, follow the steps below.

1 down

2 starting a new stroke, follow the arrow diagonally

3 follow the arrow diagonally

Next, use a pencil to trace the letter **k**.

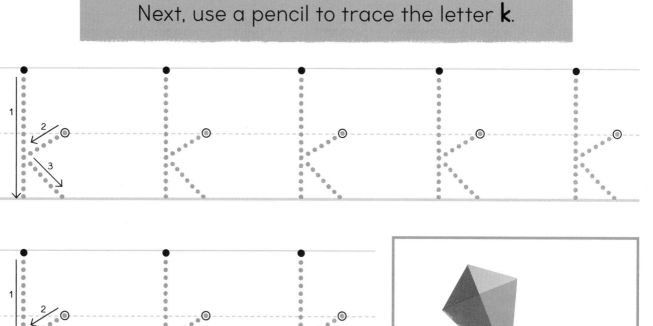

kite

Now, write the letter **k** yourself.

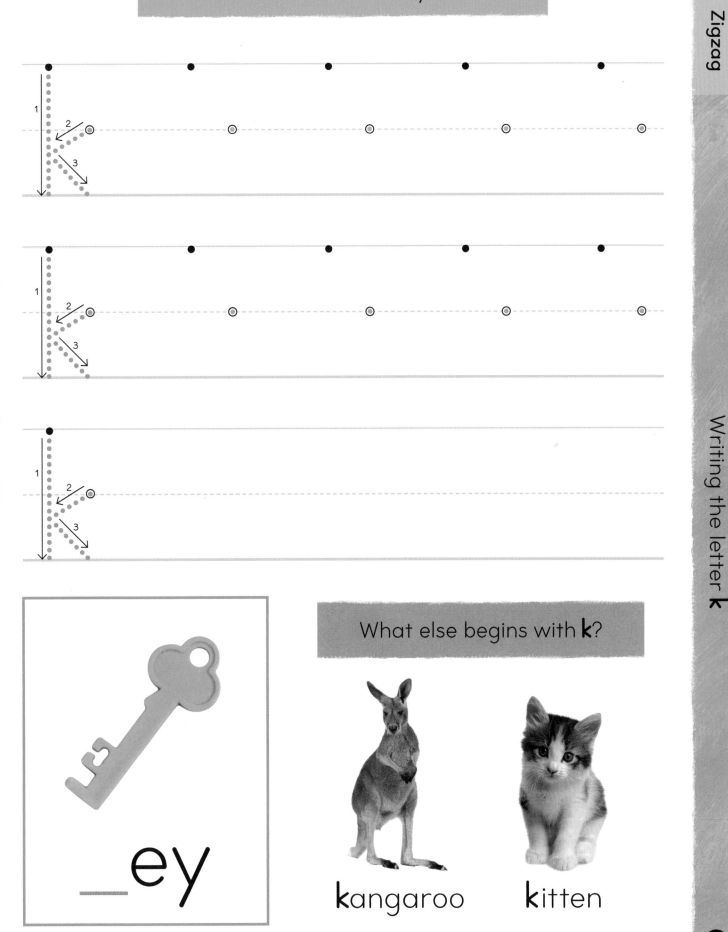

What else begins with **k**?

_ey

kangaroo   kitten

Writing the letter l

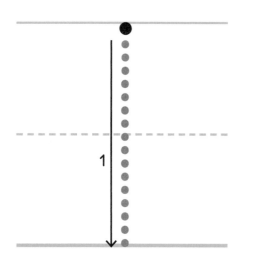

First, trace the letter l with your finger. Starting on the black dot, follow the steps below.

 **1** down

Next, use a pencil to trace the letter l.

lion

Now, write the letter l yourself.

1

1

1

_og

What else begins with l?

leaf   lemon

Writing the letter **m**

First, trace the letter **m** with your finger. Starting on the black dot, follow the steps below.

1 down
2 back up
3 around and down
4 back up
5 around and down

Next, use a pencil to trace the letter **m**.

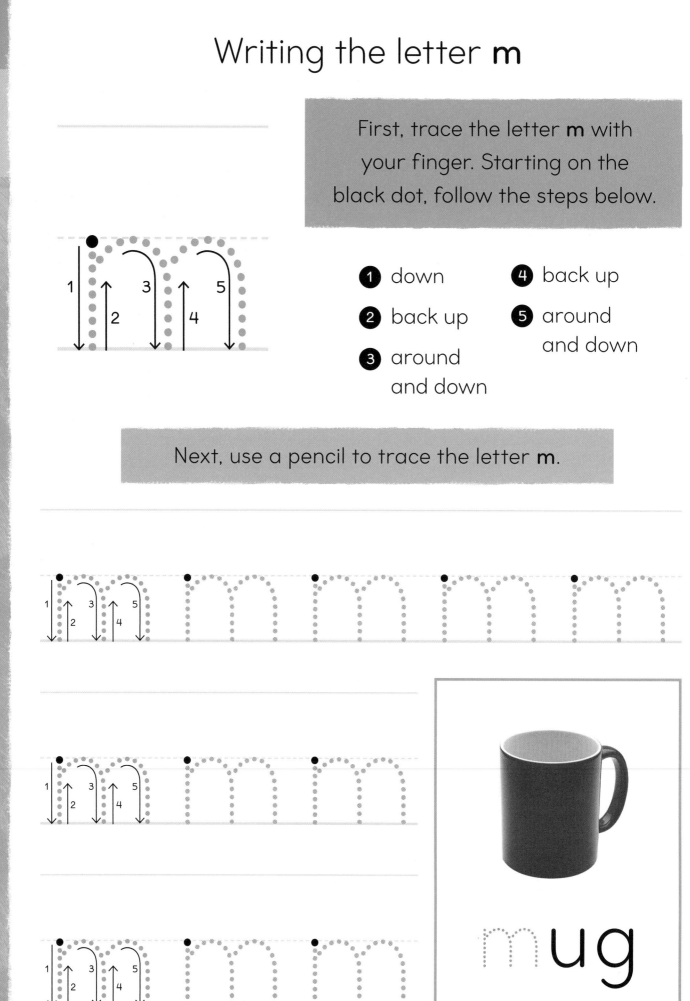

mug

Now, write the letter **m** yourself.

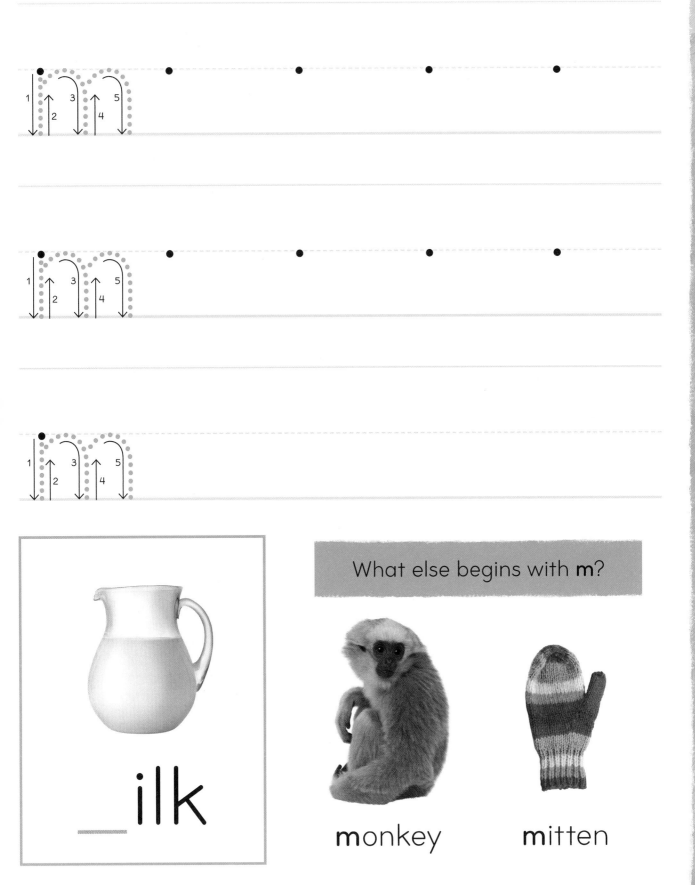

_ilk

What else begins with **m**?

monkey   mitten

Writing the letter n

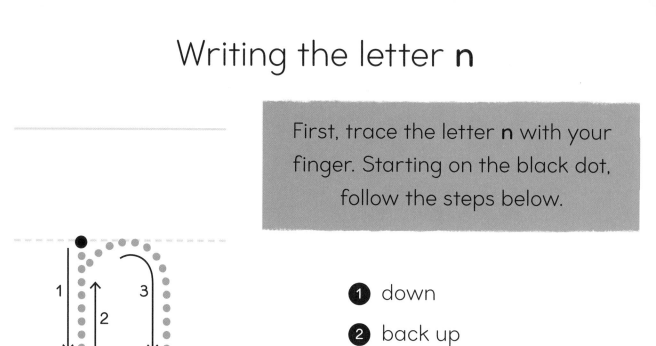

First, trace the letter **n** with your finger. Starting on the black dot, follow the steps below.

1 down

2 back up

3 around and down

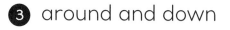

Next, use a pencil to trace the letter **n**.

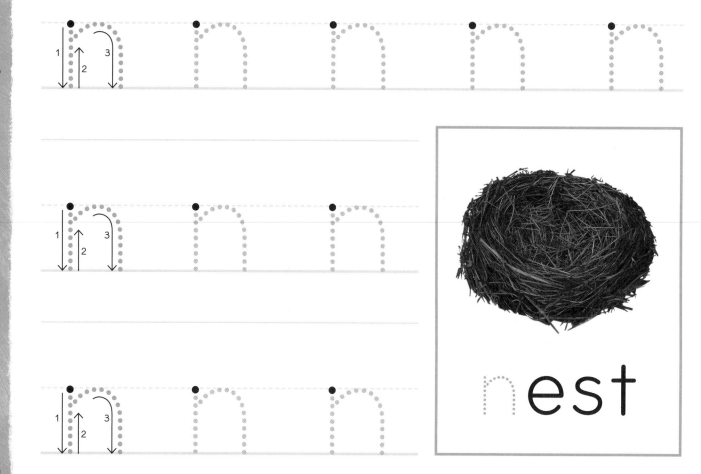

nest

Now, write the letter **n** yourself.

_et

What else begins with **n**?

nurse   **n**ecklace

Writing the letter o

First, trace the letter **o** with your finger. Starting on the black dot, follow the steps below.

1 curl all the way around to join

Next, use a pencil to trace the letter **o**.

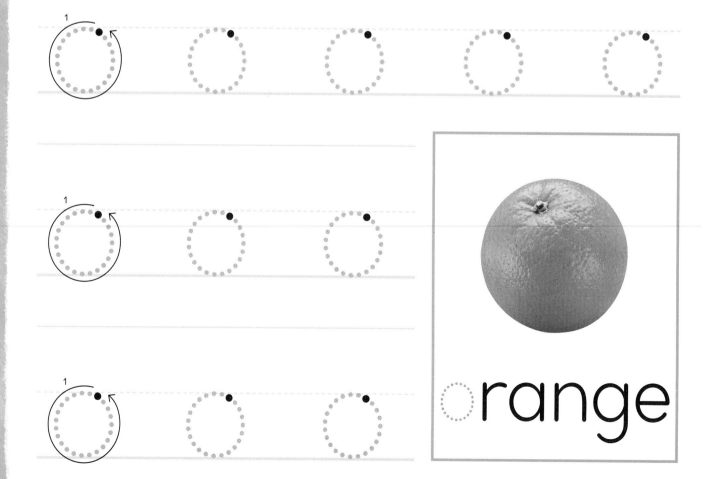

orange

Now, write the letter **o** yourself.

_tter

What else begins with **o**?

ostrich **o**ctopus

Writing the letter p

First, trace the letter **p** with your finger. Starting on the black dot, follow the steps below.

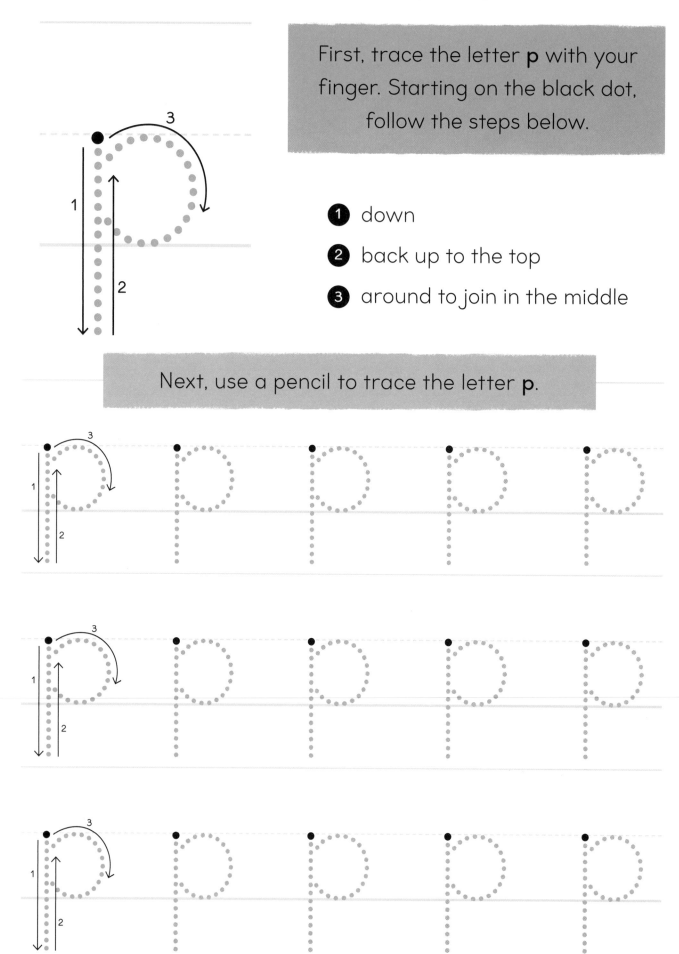

1 down

2 back up to the top

3 around to join in the middle

Next, use a pencil to trace the letter **p**.

Now, write the letter **p** yourself.

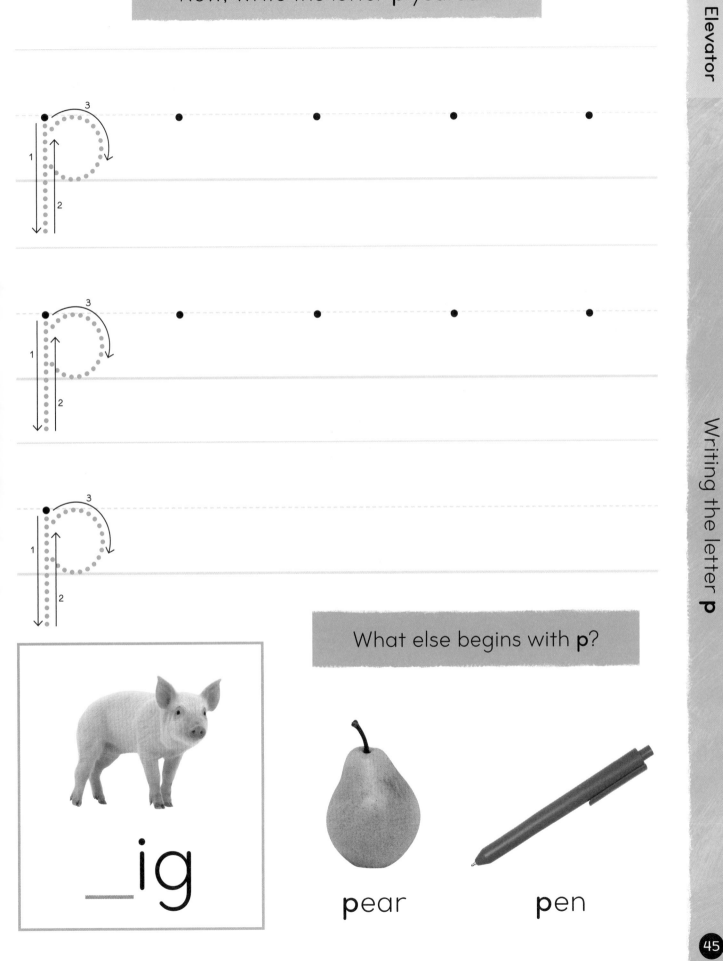

What else begins with **p**?

_ig

pear

pen

Writing the letter q

First, trace the letter **q** with your finger. Starting on the black dot, follow the steps below.

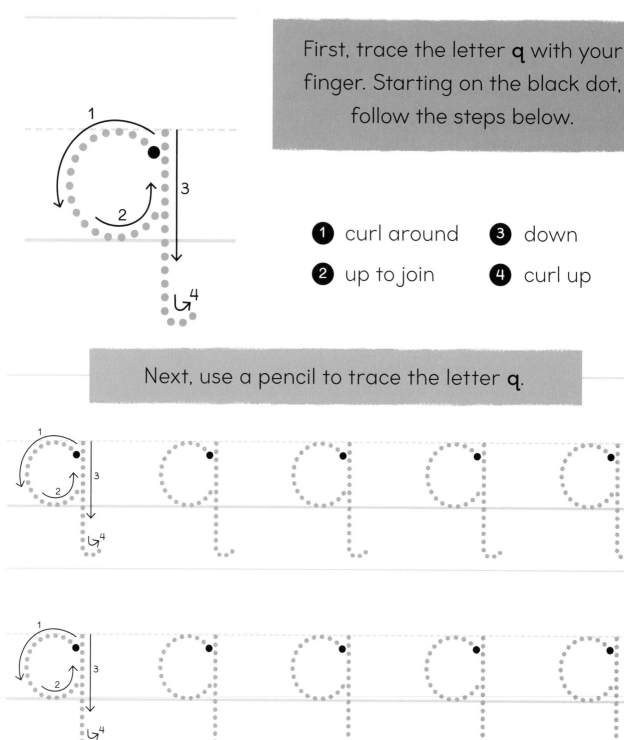

1 curl around **3** down

2 up to join **4** curl up

Next, use a pencil to trace the letter **q**.

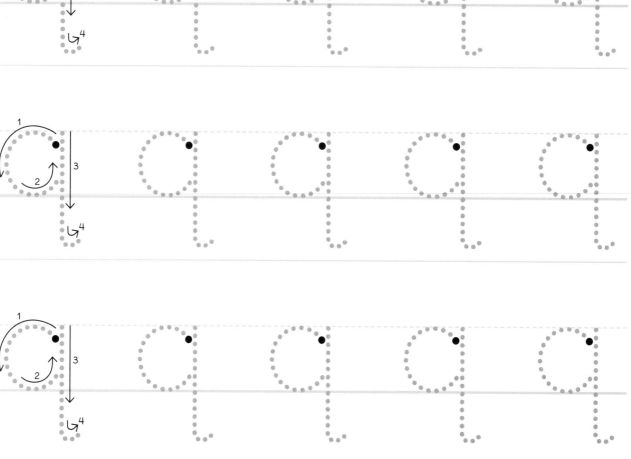

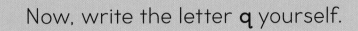

Now, write the letter **q** yourself.

What else begins with **q**?

quilt

queen

quarter

Writing the letter **r**

First, trace the letter **r** with your finger. Starting on the black dot, follow the steps below.

1 down

2 back up

3 around

Next, use a pencil to trace the letter **r**.

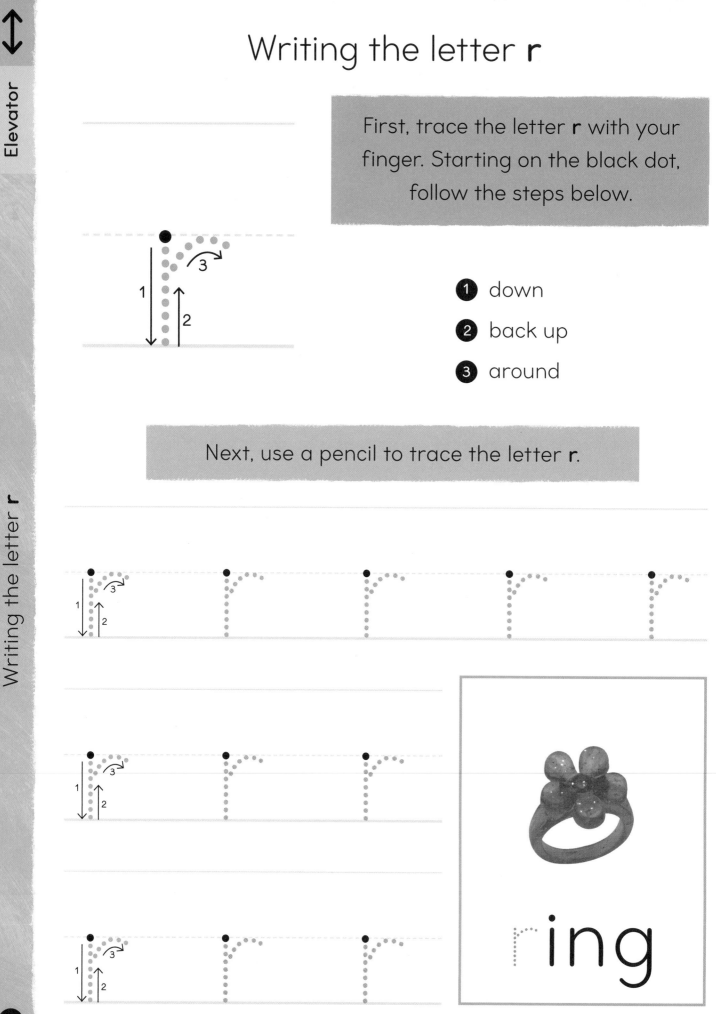

ring

Now, write the letter **r** yourself.

_obot

What else begins with **r**?

rainbow   **r**abbit

Writing the letter s

First, trace the letter **s** with your finger. Starting on the black dot, follow the steps below.

1 curl around following the arrow

Next, use a pencil to trace the letter **s**.

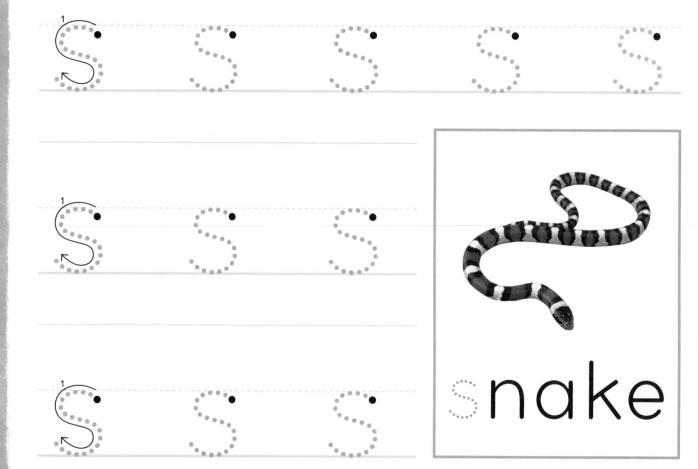

nake

Now, write the letter **s** yourself.

snail

What else begins with **s**?

sandwich   **s**tar

Writing the letter t

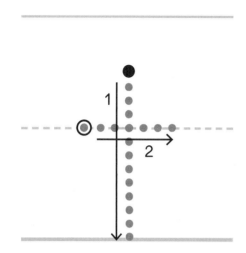

First, trace the letter **t** with your finger. Starting on the black dot, follow the steps below.

1 down

2 starting a new stroke, follow the arrow across

Next, use a pencil to trace the letter **t**.

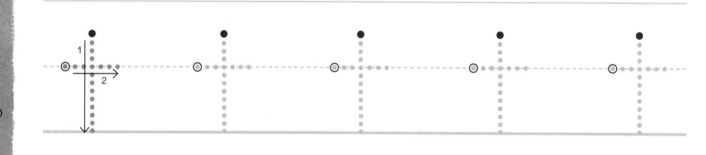

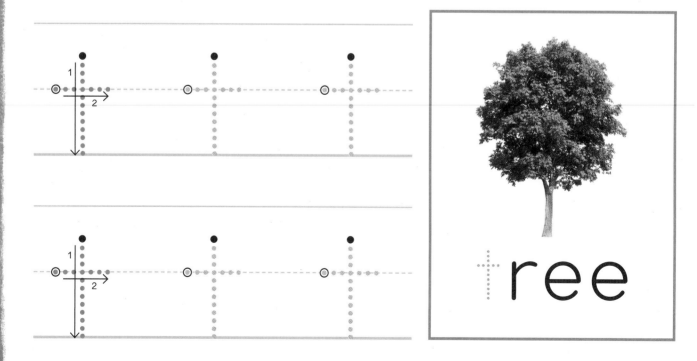

tree

Now, write the letter **t** yourself.

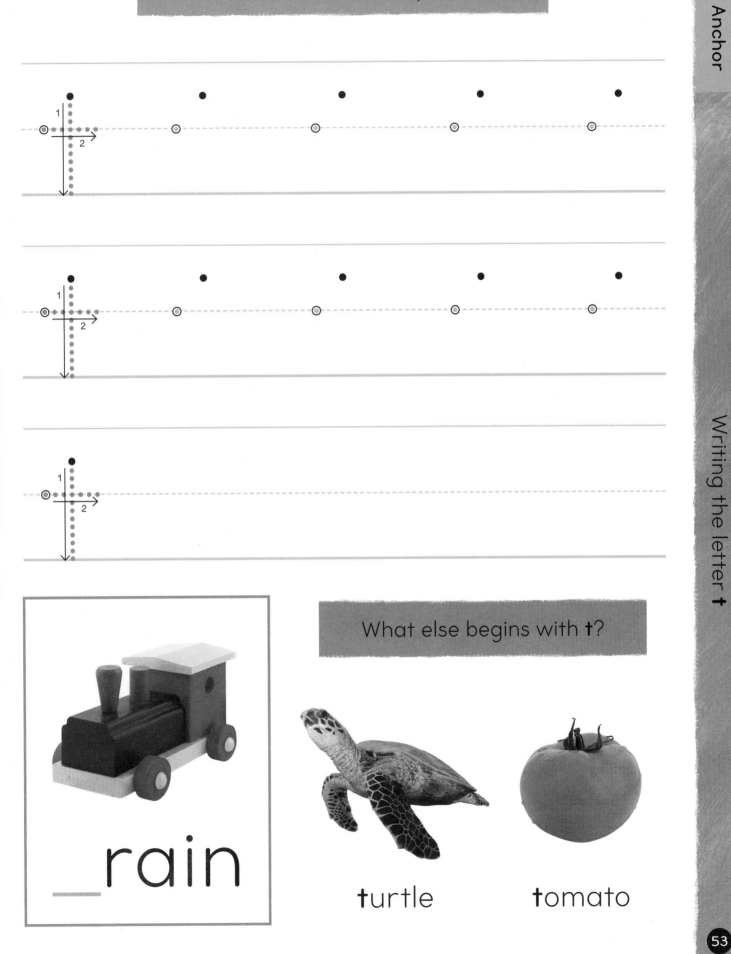

What else begins with **t**?

_rain

turtle

tomato

Writing the letter **u**

First, trace the letter **u** with your finger. Starting on the black dot, follow the steps below.

1 down

2 around and up

3 back down

Next, use a pencil to trace the letter **u**.

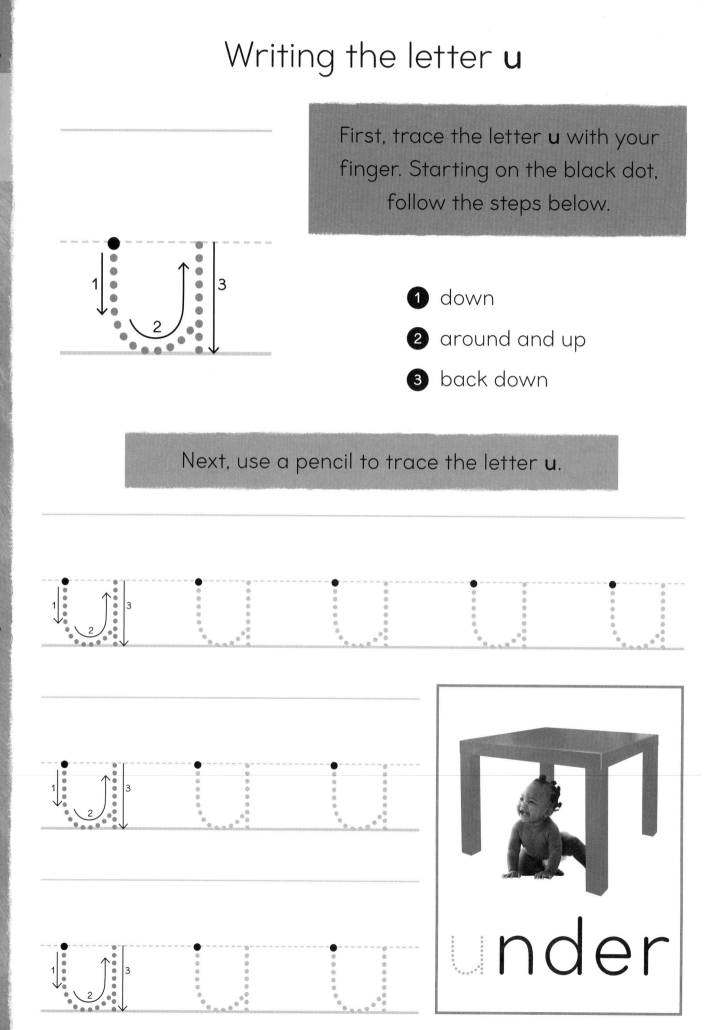

under

Now, write the letter **u** yourself.

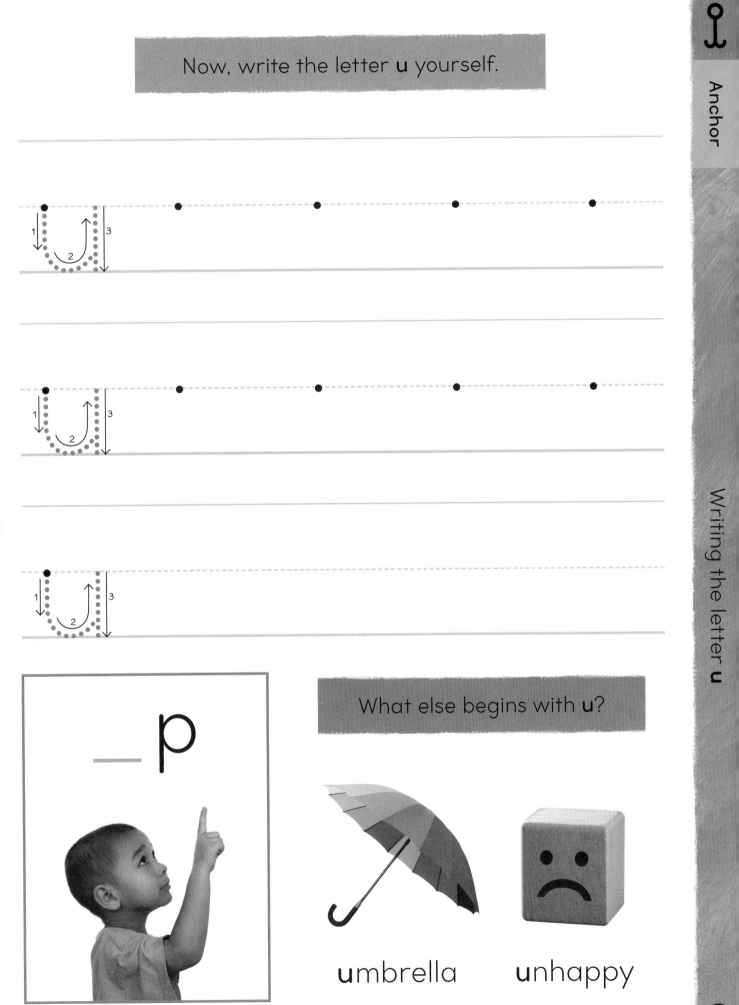

_p

What else begins with **u**?

umbrella   unhappy

Writing the letter v

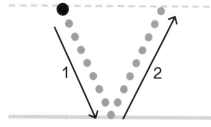

First, trace the letter **v** with your finger. Starting on the black dot, follow the steps below.

1 down diagonally

2 up diagonally

Next, use a pencil to trace the letter **v**.

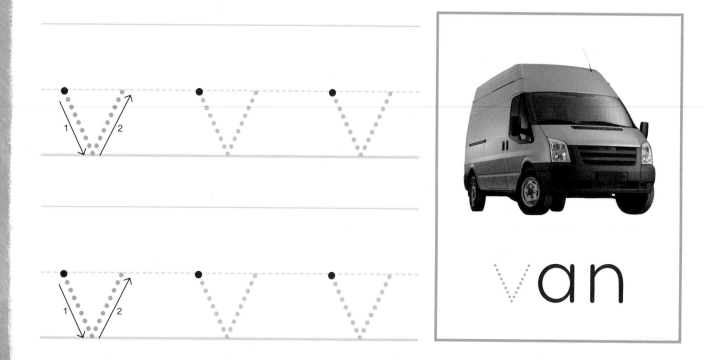

van

56

Now, write the letter v yourself.

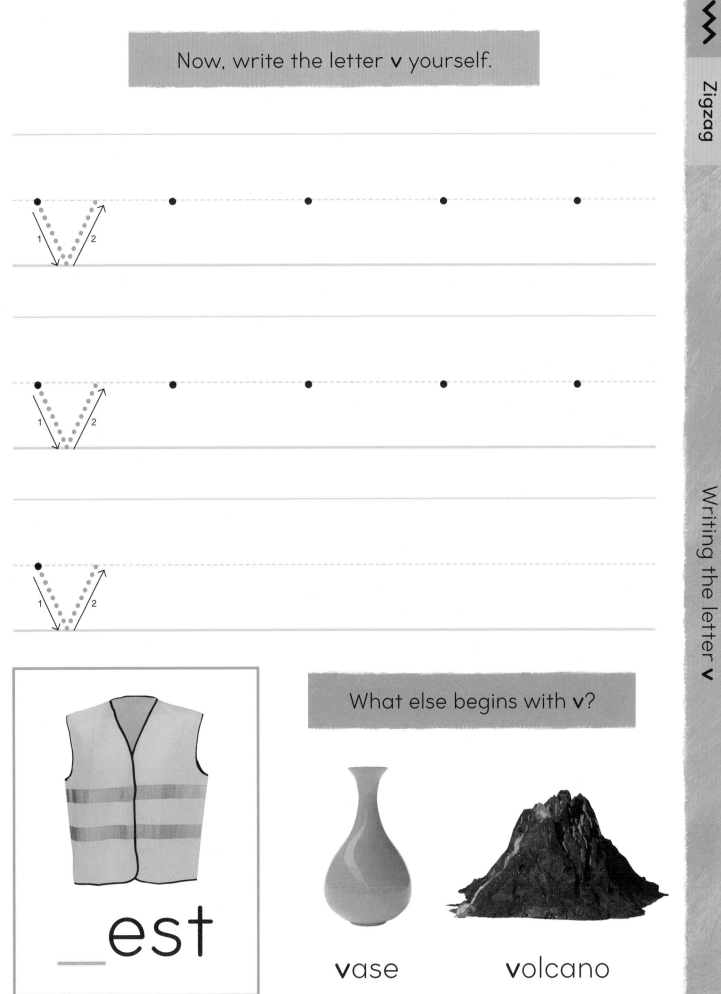

_est

What else begins with v?

vase   volcano

Writing the letter **w**

Writing the letter **w**

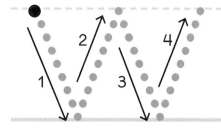

First, trace the letter **w** with your finger. Starting on the black dot, follow the steps below.

1 down diagonally

2 up diagonally

3 down diagonally

4 up diagonally

Next, use a pencil to trace the letter **w**.

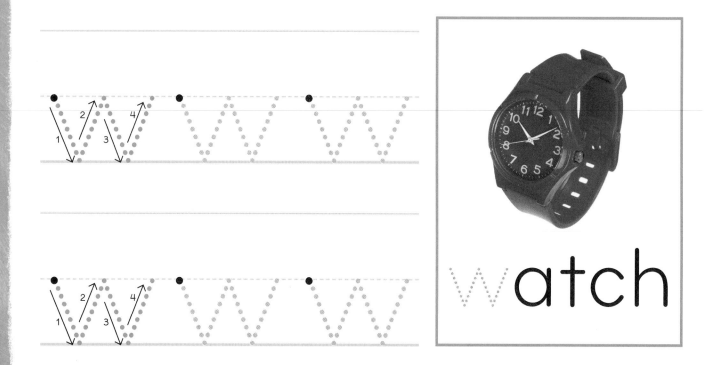

watch

Now, write the letter **w** yourself.

What else begins with **w**?

_eb

worm   **w**atermelon

Writing the letter x

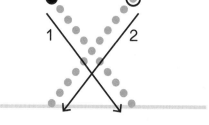

First, trace the letter **x** with your finger. Starting on the black dot, follow the steps below.

1 down diagonally

2 starting a new stroke, follow the arrow down diagonally

Next, use a pencil to trace the letter **x**.

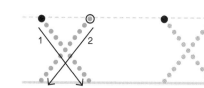

Which words end with **x**?

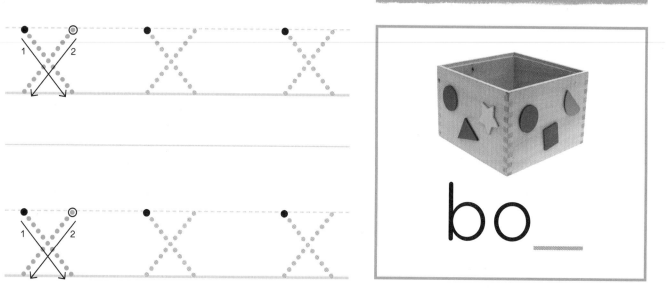

bo_

Now, write the letter **x** yourself.

Which words begin with **x**?

fo**x**

xylophone   **x**-ray

Writing the letter y

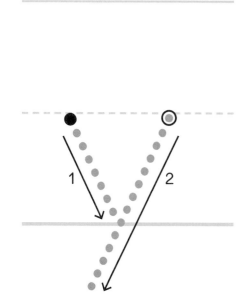

First, trace the letter **y** with your finger. Starting on the black dot, follow the steps below.

1 down diagonally

2 starting a new stroke, follow the arrow down diagonally

Next, use a pencil to trace the letter **y**.

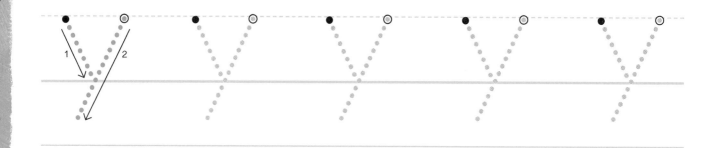

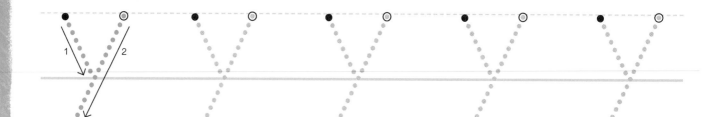

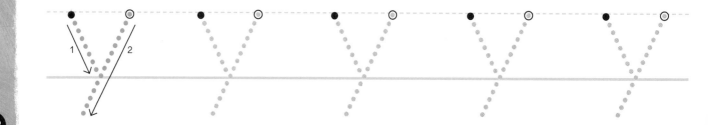

Now, write the letter **y** yourself.

What else begins with **y**?

_ak

yo-yo

yarn

Writing the letter z

First, trace the letter **z** with your finger. Starting on the black dot, follow the steps below.

1 across

2 down diagonally

3 across

Next, use a pencil to trace the letter **z**.

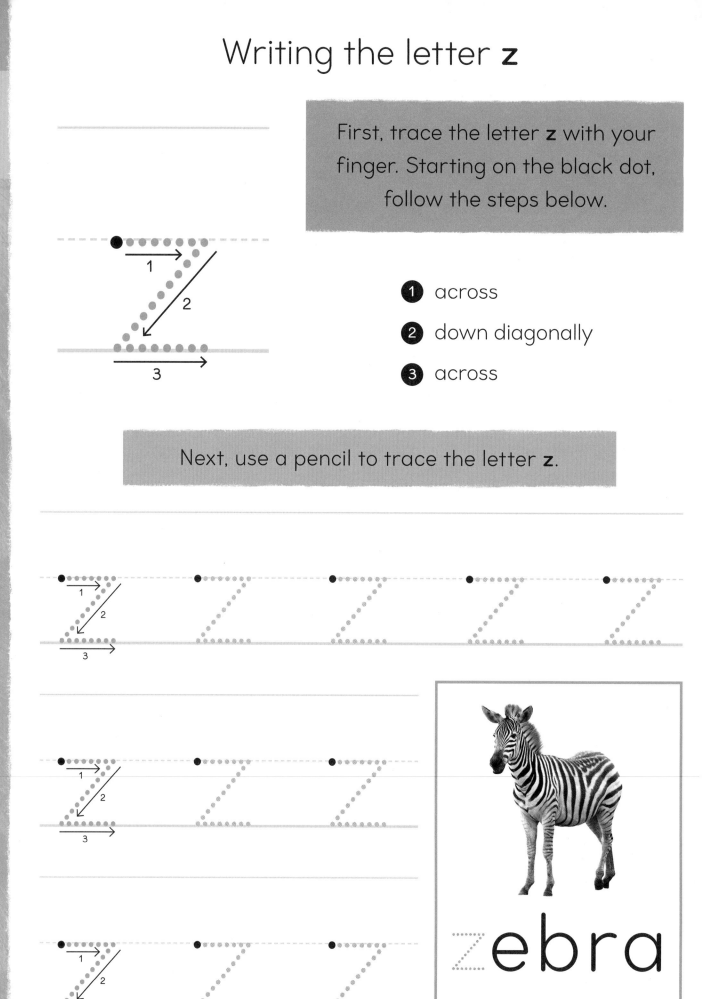

zebra

Now, write the letter **z** yourself.

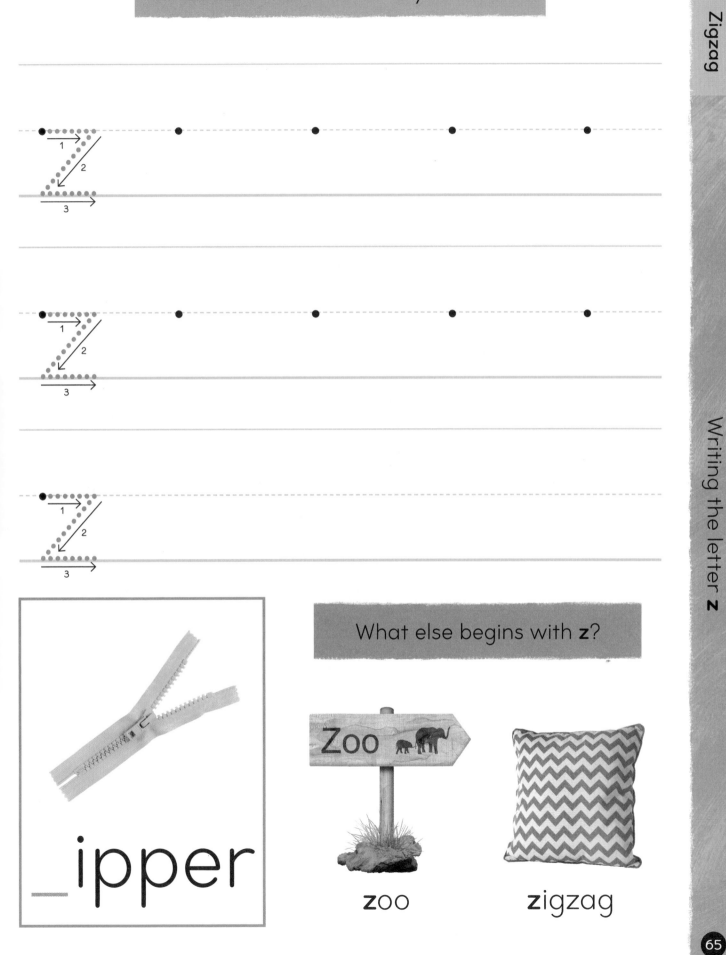

What else begins with **z**?

_ipper

zoo

zigzag

Writing the alphabet

Now that you've learned how to write every letter in the alphabet, can you write them in order?

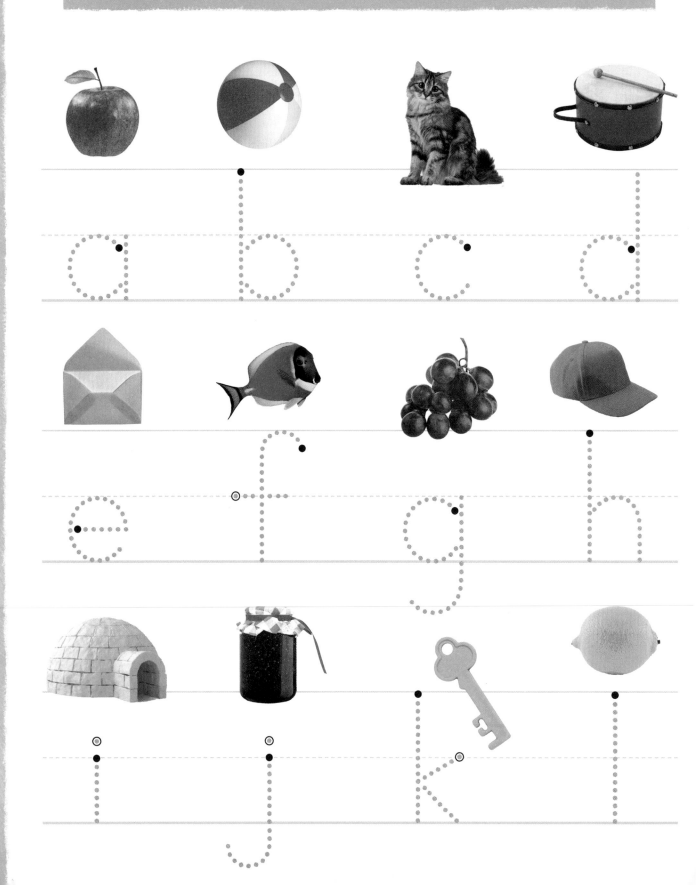

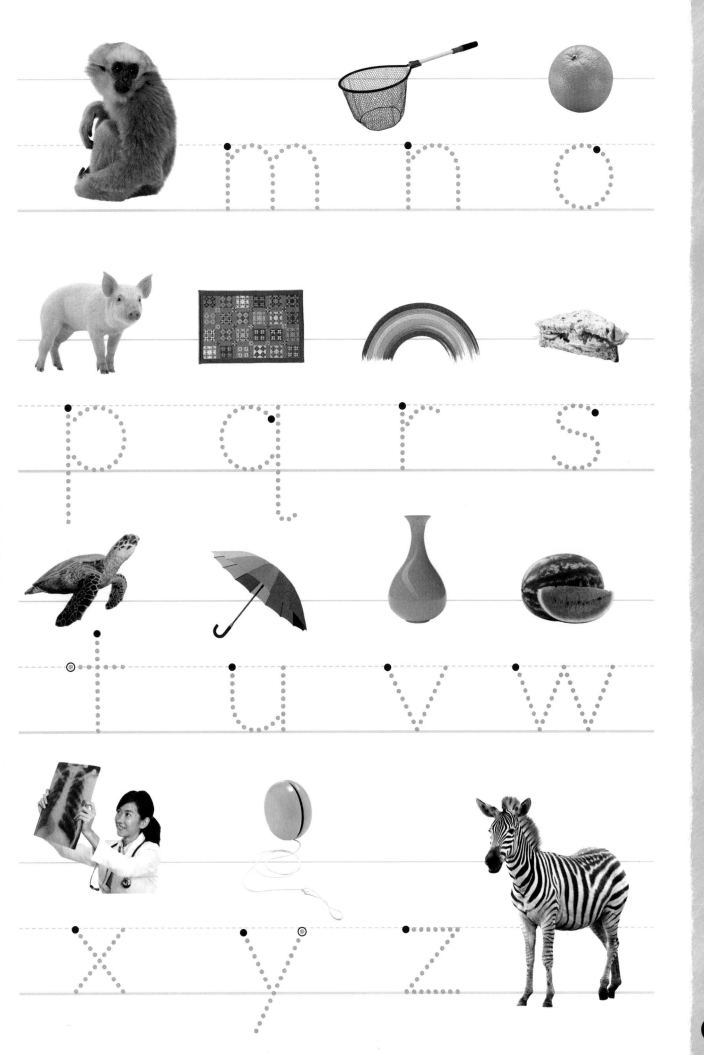

m n o

p q r s

t u v w

x y z

Writing practice
Now trace some of the new words
you have learned!

apple

yo-yo

van

box

queen

dog

milk

jam

cat

web

fish

zipper

key

ring

a b c d e f g h i j k l m
n o p q r s t u v w x y z

Can you remember some of the words you learned? Practice writing them here, using the letters above to help you. Remember to follow the lines and form the letters carefully.

Capital letters

Capital letters are used for the first letter of your name. They are also used for the first letter of a word when you write a new sentence. Practice tracing capital letters!

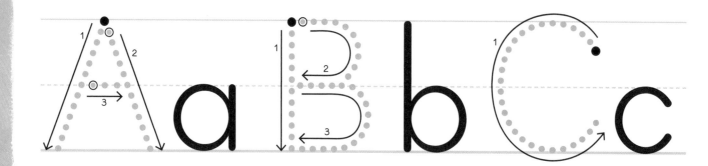

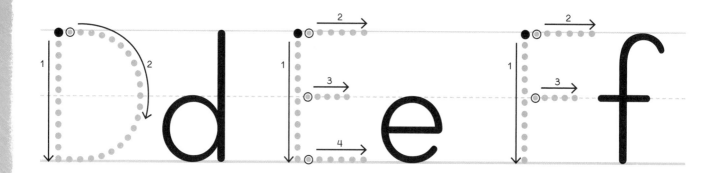

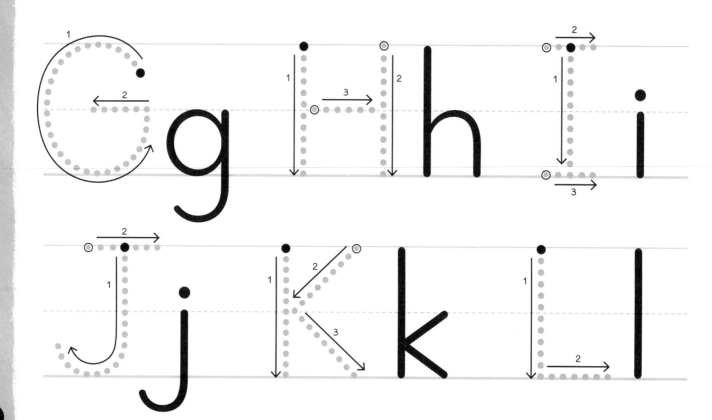

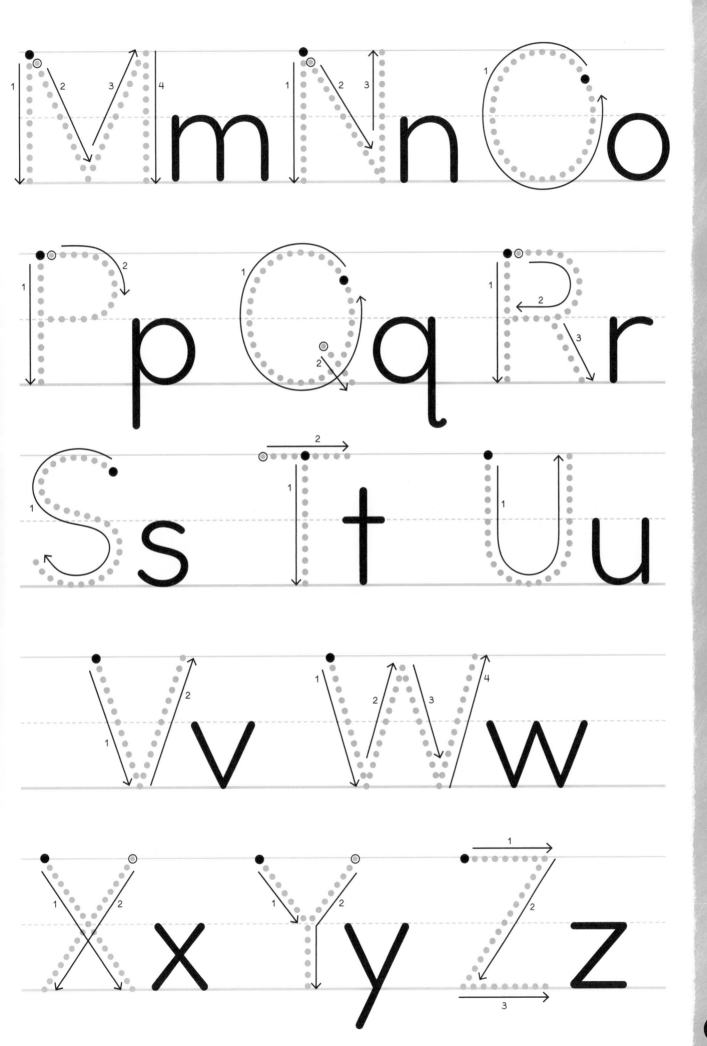

Writing your name

Ask someone to write your
name below.

Now practice writing your name.
Remember to start with a capital letter,
and write the rest in lowercase letters.

Writing numbers

Now try writing the numbers **1** through **10**.
Start on the black dot and follow the arrows.

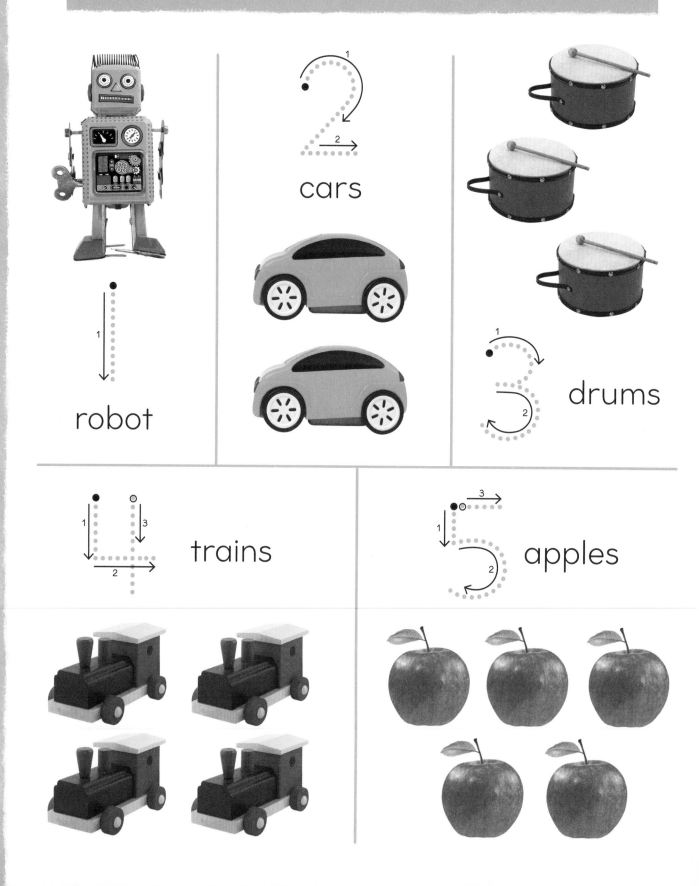

robot

cars

drums

trains

apples

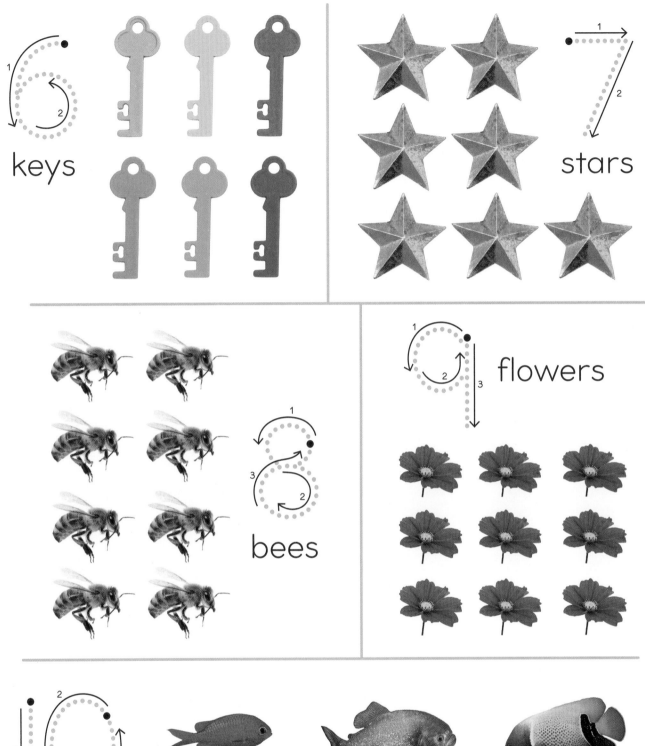

keys

stars

bees

flowers

fish

How old are you?

Now that you've learned how to write numbers, write your age below!

I am ☐ years old.

Draw a picture of yourself.

Certificate of Achievement

Great job!

This certificate is awarded to:

For successfully learning to write!

Age: _____

Date: _____

Signed: _____